Financial Crises and Asia

Financial Crises and Asia

This is a report of a conference organized by CEPR and funded
by the UK Foreign and Commonwealth Office; HM Treasury; the
Bank of England; and the Global Economic Institutions (GEI)
Research Programme (funded by the Economic Social Research
Council). The conference was hosted by the Bank of England in
London, February 1998.

Centre for Economic Policy Research

The Centre for Economic Policy Research is a network of over 350 Research Fellows, based primarily in European universities. The Centre coordinates its Fellows' research activities and communicates their results to the public and private sectors. CEPR is an entrepreneur, developing research initiatives with the producers, consumers and sponsors of research. Established in 1983, CEPR is a European economics research organization with uniquely wide-ranging scope and activities.

CEPR is a registered educational charity. Institutional (core) finance for the Centre is provided by major grants from the Economic and Social Research Council, under which an ESRC Resource Centre operates within CEPR; the Esmée Fairbairn Charitable Trust; the Bank of England; the European Monetary Institute and the Bank for International Settlements; 21 national central banks and 37 companies. None of these organizations gives prior review to the Centre's publications, nor do they necessarily endorse the views expressed therein.

The Centre is pluralist and non-partisan, bringing economic research to bear on the analysis of medium- and long-run policy questions. CEPR research may include views on policy, but the Executive Committee of the Centre does not give prior review to its publications, and the Centre takes no institutional policy positions. The opinions expressed in this report are those of the authors and not those of the Centre for Economic Policy Research.

Contents

List of Participants   **ix**

Preface   **xiii**

Conference Report

Financial Crises: The Lessons of Asia

Robert Chote   **1**

Summaries of Conference Presentations

A New Approach to Managing Financial Crises

Barry Eichengreen & Richard Portes   **35**

Currency Crisis Contagion and Containment: A Framework

Charles Wyplosz   **39**

Assessing Emerging Market Currency Risk

Manmohan Kumar & William Perraudin   **44**

Early Warning Indicators of Currency and Banking Crises in
Emerging Economies

Morris Goldstein   **48**

Macroeconomic Dimensions of the East Asian Crisis

Joseph Stiglitz   **54**

List of Participants

Beatriz Armendariz de Aghion, *University College London*

Vicki Barnett, *Financial Times*

Christopher Bliss, *University of Oxford*

Simon Brooks, *HM Treasury*

Stéphane Brunet, *Banque Nationale de Paris*

Ravi Bulchanandi, *Morgan Stanley*

Stefano Carcascio, *Banca d'Italia*

Robert Chote, *Financial Times*

Benoît Coeuré, *Ministère des Finances, Paris*

Stephen Cook, *UK Foreign and Commonwealth Office*

Hannah Corbett, *UK Foreign and Commonwealth Office*

Jennifer Corbett, *University of Oxford and CEPR*

John Drage, *Bank of England*

Barry Eichengreen, *International Monetary Fund, University of California, Berkeley and CEPR*

Huw Evans, *Bank of England*

David Folkerts-Landau, *Deutsche Morgan Grenfell*

Vítor Gaspar, *Banco de Portugal*

Francesco Giavazzi, *IGIER, Università Bocconi, Milan and CEPR*

Morris Goldstein, *Institute for International Economics*

Kevin Grice, *American Express Bank Ltd*

Lazlo Halpern, *Hungarian Academy of Science*

Peter Hamilton, *Bank of England*

Olivier Jeanne, *Ecole Nationale des Ponts et Chaussées, Paris, and CEPR*

Giles Keating, *Credit Suisse First, Boston*

Manmohan Kumar, *Credit Suisse First, Boston*

Rory Macmillan, *Debevoise & Plimpton*

Ian Michael, *Bank of England*

Colin Miles, *Bank of England*

Marcus Miller, *University of Warwick and CEPR*

Michael Mussa, *International Monetary Fund*

Tessa Ogden, *CEPR*

William Perraudin, *Birkbeck College, London and CEPR*

Richard Portes, *London Business School and CEPR*

Hélène Rey, *London School of Economics*

Jim Rollo, *UK Foreign and Commonwealth Office*

Mark Salmon, *City University Business School and CEPR*

Kim Schoenholtz, *Salomon Brothers International Limited*

Andrew Scott, *London Business School and CEPR*

Mike Stephenson, *Bank of England*

Joseph Stiglitz, *World Bank*

Dean Stokes, *HM Treasury*

Mark Taylor, *University of Oxford and CEPR*

David Vines, *University of Oxford and CEPR*

Axel Weber, *Universität Bonn and CEPR*

William White, *Bank for International Settlements*

Martin Wolf, *Financial Times*

Richard H Woodworth, *Merrill Lynch*

Charles Wyplosz, *Graduate Institute of International Studies, Geneva and CEPR*

Preface

The Asian financial crises are not the first nor the last. In an economy with no corporate bankruptcies, capital markets are not functioning well. Investors should take risks. Built into the return on investment is a premium that assumes that some proportion of investment decisions will prove mistaken and will fail. If none fail, investors have been too conservative. Many profitable - though risky - opportunities have not been exploited. This is why we have domestic bankruptcy laws that provide for 'orderly workouts' when investments and the firms that made them do fail.

Similarly, if the international capital markets are functioning well, from time to time mistakes will be made. Then one or another country (or its private sector borrowers) will fail. This country will experience a financial crisis. History records many such events. We should not expect or even wish to prevent them all. That would be possible only with insufficient, excessively risk-averse investment.

Policies and institutions should therefore aim to avoid the avoidable, but not at any cost. At one extreme, closing off international capital markets with pervasive controls would prevent international financial crises, but that would shut down one of the main engines of economic growth. At the other extreme, however, premature or poorly prepared, inadequately regulated financial liberalisation can easily lead to financial crises. International lending can be dangerous. Timely information for policy-makers and the markets can reduce the dangers. So can appropriate supervision and regulation of financial institutions.

When financial crises do occur, however, there may be extensive repercussions on the real economy and international contagion effects. It may be possible to limit or mitigate the domestic and international consequences of an individual country's financial disturbances with suitable institutions, workout procedures, and the help of international institutions like the IMF. The extent of the damage at home and international contagion will depend on the specific characteristics of the crisis.

The conference CEPR organized, which is reported in this publication, addressed both the specificities of the Asian financial crises and the more general lessons to be learned from them. From 'early warning indicators' to contagion, then to 'orderly workouts', our speakers and the discussion covered with exceptional breadth and depth the unfolding Asian crises. We were fortunate to have Robert Chote, Economics Editor of the *Financial Times*, to report the proceedings, which we believe will be valuable for both researchers and decision-makers.

This Conference Report contains summaries of five of the seven presentations given. None of the discussants' comments are published here, but some, of the many, issues raised are discussed by Robert Chote in his Report, 'Financial Crises: The Lessons of Asia'.

The conference took place on 4-5 February 1998 at the Bank of England. CEPR is very grateful to the Bank for hosting the workshop. We also wish to express our appreciation for the financial support from the UK Foreign and Commonwealth Office, HM Treasury, the Bank of England, and the Global Economic Institutions (GEI) Research programme funded by the Economic and Social Research Council. It was possible to organise this meeting in such a timely fashion only with the help of CEPR staff, among whom CEPR Chief Operating Officer, Tessa Ogden, and Programme Officer, Kate Millward, played key roles. I thank them for their very hard and effective work.

The usefulness of this report is partly a function of the exceptional speed and care with which it has been produced. For that thanks go to Sue Chapman, Publications Manager of CEPR, and her colleagues.

I am especially grateful for cooperation throughout to Jim Rollo of the UK Foreign and Commonwealth Office; it was, as always, a great pleasure to work so constructively with him.

Richard Portes
President, Centre for Economic Policy Research

6 March 1998

Financial Crises: The Lessons of Asia

Robert Chote

*"All happy families resemble one another,
but each unhappy family is unhappy in its own way."*

Leo Tolstoy (*Anna Karenina*)

Introduction

Michel Camdessus, the Managing Director of the International
Monetary Fund, described the Mexican peso collapse of 1994-5
and the international rescue effort that it prompted as 'the first
financial crisis of the 21st century'. Little did he realise that with
the millennium still a couple of years away, it would be followed
quite so soon by so many more. Numerous countries have been
affected by this outbreak of 'Asian flu', notably Indonesia, South
Korea, and Thailand, which together have required unprecedented
promises of international financial assistance exceeding $120bn.

The Asian flu took hold first in Thailand, where the International
Monetary Fund had been nervous about the country's excessive
current account deficit and its poorly supervised financial system
since at least 1995. The IMF criticized the Thai authorities in
private, and increasingly in public, but they refused to introduce
substantive policy reforms until economic disaster had already
become inevitable. Thailand finally sought the Fund's support in
the summer of 1997, when the country's exchange rate peg to the
US dollar became unsustainable.

The devaluation of the baht triggered a process of contagion in the other Asean countries, where corporate sectors had taken advantage of exchange rates pegged to the dollar to reduce their capital costs - accumulating unhedged dollar liabilities rather than local currency debt. Shortly after the Thai devaluation, Malaysia and Indonesia floated their currencies. Taiwan devalued a few months later, putting the Korean won and Hong Kong dollar under pressure. As Asia's currencies and equity markets tumbled, the impact on share prices was felt as far afield as Russia, Hungary and Brazil. Korea and Indonesia both came to the Fund for help, but the resulting promises of financial assistance, combined with the IMF's traditional macroeconomic prescriptions - fiscal consolidation and tighter monetary policy - failed to restore confidence in the financial markets. Eventually the international community was forced to accelerate the disbursement of financial help to Korea and to put pressure on commercial banks to roll over their loans to the country. Indonesia, meanwhile, was forced into a de facto debt moratorium in January.

In November 1997 US President Bill Clinton had characterised the Asian financial crises as 'a few small glitches in the road', but he was not alone in underestimating their eventual breadth and depth. In their impact on equity markets and exchange rates these crises constitute the most severe regional financial disruption since the Latin American debt crisis of 1982 and perhaps since the Creditanstalt default of 1931. By early February 1998, equity markets in Indonesia, Malaysia, the Philippines, South Korea and Thailand had declined by 53% to 76% from their 1996 or 1997 peaks in local currency terms. Meanwhile the exchange rates in these 'crisis economies' fell by 40% to 72%, measured in US dollars per unit of domestic currency.

The implications for real economic performance have also been severe. In a specially updated *World Economic Outlook* produced in December 1997 - the first such exercise to be undertaken since the aftermath of the stock market crash a decade ago - the International Monetary Fund slashed its growth forecasts for these five economies in 1998 from the 6-8% expected before the summer to 0-4%. Private sector forecasts suggest there are further downgrades to come, with outright recessions looking probable this year in Thailand, Indonesia and South Korea.

The economic effects of the crisis will not be confined to emerging Asia, even if the market turbulence turns out to have subsided for good. By December the IMF had revised down the 1998 growth forecasts it had published in May from 2.9% to 1.1% for Japan; from 5.1% to 3.5% for Latin America; and from 2.9% to 2.7% for the European Union. The crises might also pose a longer-term and more serious threat to global prosperity if protectionism flourishes as a result. A combination of depressed domestic demand and sharp devaluations means that the crisis economies will have to export their way to recovery, a process which is already taking its toll on the current account positions of their trading partners.

Real GDP Growth Forecasts for 1998 (%)

	May	October	December	February
Thailand	7.0	3.5	0	-2.7
Indonesia	7.5	6.2	2.0	-3.3
Malaysia	7.9	6.5	2.5	-3.3
Philippines	6.4	5.0	3.8	2.9
South Korea	6.3	6.0	2.5	-0.2
US	2.2	2.5	2.3	-0.2
Japan	2.9	2.1	1.1	0.1
EU	2.9	2.8	2.7	2.7

[Source: IMF *World Economic Outlook* (May, Oct, Dec) and *Consensus Economics* (Feb)]

Financial crises will always be with us, as Richard Portes and Barry Eichengreen pointed out, but no crisis is ever exactly the same as any of those which have gone before it. Taken as a group, the recent events in Asia are unusual in several respects: they have combined banking and currency crises; they have been driven by private sector behaviour rather than public sector profligacy; and they have exposed weaknesses in development models that the international community had until recently held up as models for less successful economies to emulate. The full impact of Asia's financial crises will only become clear in coming months. But they have already raised a number of issues of importance to governments, international institutions, private sector investors and financial market participants. Based primarily on the CEPR conference, 'Financial Crises and Asia', this paper explores the following issues:

1. Diagnosis: How did the financial crises arise and why did they spread from one country to the next? How do they relate to past financial crises and existing academic models of currency and banking crises?

2. Cure: Has the IMF prescribed the right medicine for the crisis economies? Are tighter monetary policy, fiscal consolidation and the closure of weak financial institutions appropriate, or do they make a bad situation worse? Has the IMF done enough to discourage excessively risky lending to emerging markets in the future? How can rescue packages minimise 'moral hazard' problems?

3. Prevention: Is it possible to devise early warning indicators that will signal when a country is vulnerable to a crisis? Had the IMF done what it could to predict and prevent crises from erupting in Asia? What policy prescriptions should it offer to other emerging market governments in order for them to avoid crises?

1. Diagnosis

In attempting to understand the genesis and development of Asia's currency crises, it is helpful to begin by examining the standard models of financial crises in the academic literature and to see what light they shed on recent events.

The so-called 'first generation' crisis models emphasise the role of excessive money-financed government borrowing, where the authorities are defending a fixed exchange rate with a limited stock of foreign exchange reserves. Profligate fiscal and monetary policies generate domestic inflation. With the nominal exchange rate fixed, this undermines competitiveness by raising the real exchange rate. This results in a widening trade deficit and an eventual recognition in the financial markets that the authorities do not possess sufficient reserves to maintain the exchange rate peg. When the stock of reserves falls to some critical level, the attempts of investors to anticipate the inevitable devaluation generate a successful speculative attack in the form of capital outflows.

The first generation models provide a reasonable explanation of many emerging market currency crises over the past two decades, including the collapse of the Mexican peso three years ago. But the first generation models could not explain the de facto collapse of the European exchange rate mechanism in 1992-3. The member countries of the ERM had not been fiscally profligate, nor were they running loose monetary policies. Inflation rates were also modest and current account positions appeared sustainable.

Economists had devised 'second generation' crisis models to explain the collapse of the ERM, in which the political and economic costs of unemployment played a crucial role. Because of the asymmetric inflationary shock of German unification, the Bundesbank had to impose interest rates on the other ERM member countries that were much tighter than their domestic circumstances warranted. The second generation models assume that if the tight monetary policy required to maintain an exchange rate peg pushes up unemployment, the market will eventually deduce that the political cost of rising joblessness will outweigh the political and economic benefits of maintaining the peg. Speculation against the parity will then demand further interest rate increases to defend it, which the markets will regard as increasingly untenable. Speculation will therefore intensify until the authorities give in. In second generation models, a speculative attack on a currency can therefore arise because of a predicted future deterioration in economic fundamentals or simply through a self-fulfilling prophecy.

Paul Krugman, among others, has argued that neither the first nor the second generation crisis models fit the Asian story particularly well. The first generation models seem inappropriate because the crisis economies were running neither profligate fiscal policies nor loose monetary policies. The general government sector of the five crisis economies was in surplus by about 1% of GDP on average between 1994 and 1997. They also experienced no significant acceleration in money supply or credit growth in the run-up to the crises. The rate of money supply growth was quite rapid at 18-20%, but not excessive against a background of 15% nominal GDP growth. Inflation rates were relatively stable, meanwhile, at around 6%. In the context of the second generation models, economic growth had slowed modestly but unemployment showed no signs of rising to the sorts of levels which might pose a serious political problem. Policy-makers did not, therefore, have a significant incentive to run loose policies in the future.

If there were macroeconomic warning signals for the Asian crises, they showed up in the balance of payments. The current account deficits of the crisis economies widened from 2% of GDP in 1993 to more than 5% in 1996 - Thailand saw its deficit balloon to more than 8%, having equalled or exceeded 6% in six of the past 15 years. In part this reflected the 10% to 20% appreciation in real exchange rates which the crisis economies experienced between 1994 and 1997. Gavyn Davies, at Goldman Sachs, cites several explanations for this deterioration in competitiveness: domestic inflation in excess of the world average; the rise in the US dollar to which these currencies were pegged; the depreciation of the Japanese yen; and the devaluation of the Chinese yuan in 1994. But David Folkerts-Landau argued that the 15% overvaluations typically displayed by the crisis economies were not particularly unusual or worrying. Morris Goldstein agreed that 'these were not huge misalignments, but they nevertheless increased vulnerability' when many Asian economies experienced a sharp slowdown in export receipts during 1996 as a result of slower world trade growth and an inventory glut in the global electronics industry.

Rising current account deficits may have been a warning signal, but for several years the deficits had been financed successfully by capital account inflows from overseas - so much so that it was also possible to build up foreign exchange reserves substantially. Davies calculates that the inflow of private capital into the five crisis economies averaged 5% of GDP through the 1990s, rising to 7% in 1996, but less than 1.5 percentage points of this were in the form of relatively secure net direct investment: in 1995 and 1996 inflows worth more than 4% of GDP entered via the banking sector. Non-crisis economies in Asia had smaller inflows or - in the case of China - larger ones dominated by net direct investment. Capital inflows implied a rapid build-up in the net foreign liabilities of the private sector in the crisis economies. From 1993 to 1996, the foreign liabilities of commercial banks rose by 12% a year while foreign assets rose by only about 7%. The picture was similar in the corporate sector, leaving banks and companies alike highly exposed in the event of an unexpected devaluation of the currency.

Charles Wyplosz argues that, with hindsight, it was clear from the macroeconomic indicators that Thailand at least was a basket case. But it did not seem inevitable that the other casualties should have got into trouble. It was also curious that the crises have hopped from country to country, often with weeks or months between them. Wyplosz argued that the affected countries had to have possessed some pre-existing fragility, which rendered them vulnerable to attack without necessarily determining the precise timing of the crisis. There is thus a 'grey zone' where crises may or may not occur. In Mexico, this pre-existing fragility was created by the government's decision to issue tesobonos - the dollar-linked securities that were sold in 1994 when the Colosio assassination reduced demand for traditional peso-denominated cetes securities. In Asia, the build-up of private sector dollar-denominated debt can be seen in the same way.

William Perraudin argued that while economic fundamentals might not be able to explain why a crisis takes place in a particular country at a particular time, they will help to determine the range of circumstances under which a country is vulnerable to attack. But an enormous range of factors can then be singled out as a potential source of lethal self-fulfilling attacks. And, as Michael Mussa pointed out, often the mystery is not why one country has suffered an attack under such circumstances but why another has not.

Joseph Stiglitz argued that the Asian crisis economies displayed vulnerabilities in four areas:

* weak financial sectors

* High corporate debt-to-equity ratios

* large short-term foreign denominated debts

* Lack of transparency, so that lenders had difficulty distinguishing sound from unsound institutions.

Stiglitz argued that these factors amplified the crisis when it broke, but that their severity had not changed significantly in the run-up to the crises - so they could not be cited as proximate causes. He added that policy makers should be wary of explanations relying on overheating or overinvestment. It is easy to blame overinvestment ex post, but was there overinvestment ex ante? South Korea had moderate and declining inflation in the run-up to its crisis and only a victim of paranoia would have diagnosed a serious inflation problem.

Mussa argued that the authorities in the crisis countries made the situation worse in the months running up to these crises, as they engaged in last-gasp attempts to defend their exchange rate regimes. This would not have been a problem had they succeeded, but in failing they made the situation worse than if the authorities had thrown in the towel earlier. He noted that when the Thai baht was devalued the country had $18bn in reserves and $20bn in forward commitments, but as recently as three months beforehand it had $35bn in reserves and no forward commitments. In early December 1996 South Korea appeared to have net reserves of $25-30bn, but $20-25bn had been leant to institutions that had invested them in illiquid and unusable junk paper. David Folkerts-Landau noted that the IMF's calls for 'greater exchange rate flexibility' in Thailand before the crisis broke fell on stony ground in a financial system built on local cohesiveness and long-term agreements between the key players. Martin Wolf questioned whether governments could ever be prevented from engaging in last-gasp defences of fixed exchange rate regimes, without banning currency pegs altogether.

Krugman argues that academic models focusing on currency crises miss the point in Asia. He notes that in all the afflicted countries a boom-bust cycle in asset markets preceded the currency crisis: equity and land prices soared and then plunged. In addition, financial intermediaries played a key role. In Thailand 'finance companies' borrowed dollars short term and lent them for speculative real estate investments. In South Korea it was conventional banks that borrowed dollars short-term, lending them to highly leveraged corporations to finance capital spending that created what turned out to be excess capacity in highly cyclical industries such as steel and semi-conductors:

> 'The Asian crisis is best seen not as a problem brought about by fiscal deficits, as in "first generation" models, nor as one brought on by macroeconomic temptation, as in "second

generation" models, but as one brought on by financial excess and then financial collapse. Indeed to a first approximation, currencies and exchange rates may have had little to do with it: the Asian story is really about a bubble in, and subsequent collapse of, asset values in general, with the currency crises more a symptom than a cause.'

Krugman argues that the liabilities of these financial intermediaries were perceived to enjoy an implicit government guarantee. These institutions were essentially unregulated - loan classification and provisioning practices were too lax; there was too much 'connected lending' to bank directors, managers and their related businesses; there was excessive government ownership or involvement in the institutions; and the quality of public disclosure and transparency requirements was also poor. The institutions were also not required to hold sufficient equity in their balance sheets. As a result, they were subject to a severe moral hazard problem in which the owners of the institutions were encouraged to engage in excessively risky lending in the expectation that they would be bailed out if things went wrong. Like thrifts in the US savings and loans debacle, they were able to raise money at low interest rates and lend it at premium rates to finance speculative investments. In Asia this excessively risky lending fuelled asset price inflation, creating a virtuous circle: risky lending drove up the prices of risky assets, which made the financial condition of the intermediaries seem sounder than it was, which in turn encouraged and allowed them to engage in further risky lending.

When the bubble burst, the virtuous circle became a vicious one. Falling asset prices exposed the insolvency of some of the intermediaries, forcing them to cease their operations or sell assets, which led to asset price deflation. The fall in asset prices further undermined the solvency of the intermediaries, helping to explain the depth and severity of the crisis. Marcus Miller argued that land prices were particularly important in the asset bubble story, observing that if imprudent companies went bust when the bubble burst they could bring down prudent ones too. Exposure to the property sector accounted for around a quarter of bank loans in Thailand, Indonesia and Malaysia. Stiglitz argued that liberalisation aggravated the bubble, noting that restrictions on real estate lending in Thailand were removed without improving the regulatory regime.

Although Krugman does not emphasise the role of currency crisis in his story, it is easy to see why a fall in asset prices should be accompanied by severe pressure on the exchange rate. The weakening of bank balance sheets presumably raised fears that the central bank would have to print money to recapitalise them, which would hit the exchange rate. In addition, the current account deficit would have to be corrected quickly if capital inflows dried up, again requiring a devaluation. With hindsight, Vines argued, downturns in the crisis economies would have been far less severe if lending had been securitised and their exchange rate pegs abandoned for floating rate regimes

Olivier Jeanne pointed out that events in the currency markets exacerbated the vicious circle, as depreciation raised the value of intermediaries' liabilities further above the value of their assets, contributing to more failures. Conventional wisdom suggests that the authorities should help institutions when they are temporarily illiquid, but not when they are permanently insolvent. But illiquidity and insolvency are impossible to distinguish here. Jeanne noted that economists were still trying to distinguish liquidity and solvency crises from the last century, so it was hardly surprising that the distinction was causing problems for policy-makers now. Morris Goldstein added that banks in two or three of the Asean countries were insolvent even at pre-crisis exchange and asset prices. The same is true of China's state-owned banks, which remain intact for now.

Echoing Krugman, Folkerts-Landau argued that the Asian crisis had seen a replay of the US Savings and Loans episode. Merchant banks in South Korea and finance companies in Thailand and Indonesia had enjoyed implicit guarantees. Most of those who provided these intermediaries with funds believed that they were protected from risk, an impression reinforced by the political connections of the owners of these institutions. These implicit guarantees meant that the fiscal position in crisis countries was not as good as it looked: contingent liabilities were not taken into account.

Mussa argued that the impact of the implicit guarantees was obvious in South Korea. It was clear by last summer that South Korea had $25bn in short-term debts that had to be paid by the end of the year, but only $10-2bn in usable reserves. In August the authorities guaranteed the liabilities of all Korean financial institutions and overseas subsidiaries. The policy was to pay cash to meet maturing obligations - including those of a dozen merchant banks in receivership. Not surprisingly, people rushed to claim this money before it ran out. No government will be prepared to see its core financial institutions go to the wall, but the guarantee could have been much less broad.

Asian corporates made use of the intermediaries to access credit markets. In this context Folkerts-Landau likened Peregrine, the collapsed Hong Kong investment bank to Drexel Lambert in the US: it brought high margin borrowers to market and made use of implicit guarantees. As David Hale of Kemper Zurich has argued, Peregrine's decision to lend a third of its capital to an Indonesian cab company chaired by President Suharto's daughter would in the past have been seen as seedcorn to establish profitable relationships with the whole Suharto family. Now it is seen as a symbol of the way western bankers have misjudged Asian credit risk through the lending boom. Portes notes that while some of the investment financed by capital inflows was bad because of 'crony capitalism', some was also bound to be profitable - especially at depreciated exchange rates. But depreciation meant the debt burden became unserviceable in the short term.

Genuine investment funds had been flowing into the region, but there was froth on top. In a recent paper, Takatoshi Ito and Richard Portes argue that all crises are in a sense 'crises of success', because the initial capital inflow that eventually proves unsustainable is both a sign and - for a time - a cause of economic promise and success. The problem is that countries have not yet learnt how best to cope with these inflows. In Asia one response by the intermediaries was to diversify into junk paper, so South Korean merchant banks ended up holding Brazilian and Turkish paper and Russian GKOs. Folkerts-Landau added that Japan had been used since the end of 1995 as a funding source for short-term leveraged players moving into Asia. The boards of European banks deliberately responded to squeezed margins in the early 1990s by pursuing business in 'middle market Asia'. US institutions took advantage of this to unload bad apples onto the Europeans. This left them with little exposure according to the official statistics, but they had a phenomenal leveraged exposure off balance sheet: 'If you wanted a $1bn currency put you went to a US bank, if you wanted credit you went to a European one.' Decisions to lend to Asian borrowers were also based on information far poorer than the same institutions would have required to agree a loan to a US corporate.

Once the first crisis had erupted in Thailand, why did the Asian flu spread from country to country in the way that it did? Goldstein pointed out that this contagion effect is normally greater during periods of turbulence than in periods of calm, that it operates on a regional rather than a global basis and that it usually runs from big economies to small ones. The Asian crisis is therefore unusual in that it started in a relatively small country - Thailand - and spread to both large and small economies all around the world.

Bilateral trade and investment links can be important in explaining contagion, but these relationships are too weak in the case of Thailand to provide anything like the whole story. For example, Thailand takes 5% or less of the exports of Malaysia, Singapore and the Philippines. But as contagion spread from country to country, the competitive dynamics of devaluation would have had a greater affect. What is an equilibrium exchange rate against the dollar before competitor countries devalue is unlikely to remain one afterwards. Goldstein argues that these dynamics helped explain contagion in the ERM crisis of 1992-3 and that they provide a partial explanation for the increasing pressure several countries felt after the initial devaluations of the Thai baht and Indonesian rupiah. Some observers argue that China's devaluation in 1994 may have caused the Asian crises via this route, but the large share of transactions carried out in the parallel exchange market before 1994 mean that the impact of the Chinese devaluation was unlikely to have been large enough to explain what followed.

Wyplosz argued that an 'information cascade' (or what Goldstein terms a 'wake-up call') was important in the contagion process within Asia. The situation in Thailand may have prompted international investors to reassess the creditworthiness of Asian borrowers. When they did so they would have found similar problems: weak financial sectors with poor supervision, big current account deficits, overvalued exchange rates, poor quality investment, export slowdowns and overcapacity in key industries.

2. Cure

a). Policy Prescriptions and IMF Programs

The international community has assembled unprecedented promises of financial support for the hardest hit victims of Asia's financial crises. The IMF has played a leading role in co-ordinating these packages, but it never provides financial help without strings attached. The conditions it has attached to these loans - and the tactics it has used to help resolve the crises - have been the subject of keen debate.

Some critics of IMF programs - notably Jeffrey Sachs at the Harvard Institute for International Development - argue that the Fund has exacerbated the Asian crisis by prescribing excessively contractionary monetary and fiscal policies and by mandating the closure of banks and finance companies. They point out that the public finances of the crisis countries were generally in good order, that inflation was not a problem and that bank closures can easily undermine confidence and exacerbate any credit crunch. As evidence for their case, these critics point out that the rescue packages have failed to produce a rapid turnaround in currency and equity markets. In this spirit, Wyplosz argued that it was difficult to rationalise macroeconomic retrenchment in cases where a crisis arose from self-fulfilling speculation rather than poor fundamentals.

Stiglitz noted that the crisis economies had been roughly in macroeconomic balance, but that they were now facing big falls in domestic demand and strong recessionary pressures. Exports should rise because of the sharp fall in the exchange rate, although this might be hampered by the devaluations in other crisis economies and by shortages of trade credit. If these economies were not open to capital flows the obvious policy response would be to boost domestic demand, but the situation is more complicated when capital flows have to be taken into account.

Stiglitz pointed out that opinions differed on the fiscal and monetary policies appropriate to deal with a falling currency. Economists believe that increasing budget deficits strengthens the exchange rate, while many financial market participants believe that doing so weakens the exchange rate. Conventional wisdom meanwhile suggested that higher interest rates should help appreciate the currency, but this was difficult to rationalise if people knew that the rise in interest rates would be temporary. He noted that there had been no significant correlation between changes in interest rates and changes in the exchange rate during the Mexican crisis and its aftermath. In addition rises in interest rates were more likely to exacerbate financial sector weakness than falls in the exchange rate. So why impose higher interest rates on crisis countries?

Stiglitz argued that if crisis countries wish to attract capital flows back to their shores, then it is the certainty-equivalent rate of return available to investors that matters. This in turn depends on four factors: the interest rate, the probability of repayment, the expected change in the exchange rate and the risk premium. Stiglitz argued that raising interest rates could reduce the certainty-equivalent rate of return, because it might increase the chances of default - especially in economies with high debt-to-equity ratios and weak financial systems. If they threatened to raise unemployment, higher interest rates might also increase the risk premium by threatening social and political unrest. The bottom line, he argued, was that tightening monetary and fiscal policies might deter capital inflows by reducing the expected rate of return.

Francesco Giavazzi argued that the impact of changes in the budget deficit on the exchange rate was not in doubt: if the markets expected a widening budget deficit to be monetised, then it would weaken the exchange rate, but if they did not expect it to be monetised, then it would strengthen the exchange rate. He added that the impact of an increase in interest rates on the currency would depend on whether the financial markets believed that it could be sustained, noting that Argentina and Hong Kong had managed to sustain high interest rates for relatively long periods.

Mussa conceded that creation of any IMF program was a bizarre undertaking with an air of unreality surrounding it. He argued that it was important to understand how programs evolved, citing the Thai program as an example. The IMF had seen the Thai program coming in advance, having pressed the authorities to change their approach to the exchange rate in autumn 1996 and more aggressively by the following spring. By the time the Thais came to the Fund for help in July, their reserves had been blown away.

Any IMF program involves a set of macroeconomic assumptions. In the first round it was assumed that economic growth would slow from a potential rate of 7% or 8% to 3.5% in 1997 and 2.5% in 1998. The current account deficit was 8% of GDP, but private capital flows looked unlikely to finance a deficit of more than 4%. The Fund felt it was appropriate for the public sector to contribute to narrowing the current account deficit by reducing the budget deficit. Fiscal consolidation was also justified by the need to pay some of the costs of financial sector restructuring. IMF staff in Washington wanted a fiscal contraction of 3-4% of GDP, but the staff in the field found the authorities reluctant to go above 2%. This gap was finessed by agreeing a contingency plan for extra consolidation if growth fell short of the figure assumed in the program - which many Fund staff expected anyway. The measures amounted to 3% of GDP including this contingency element, but this did not take into account the quasi-fiscal losses which turned out to be hidden in the public sector's balance sheet.

By this stage the baht had depreciated to around 30 to the dollar, which at the time looked excessive. So the Fund urged the authorities to raise interest rates to 25%, against a background in which inflation was expected to rise from around 5% to around 10%. The Fund also demanded suspension of several finance companies. Monetary conditions were indeed tightened, but the Bank of Thailand soon backed off. There was also weak implementation of structural reforms, because of divisions in the governing coalition and political pressures to keep the finance companies afloat. These reverses both undermined confidence in the program and the baht suffered as a result. 'The consequence of backing away is reliably catastrophic', Mussa argued. 'If you show cowardice in the face of the enemy, you are finished.'

Missions returned to Thailand in the autumn to secure greater fiscal tightening. Arguably the magnitude of the second round of fiscal tightening was excessive, although some extra consolidation would certainly have been needed to sustain confidence. The Thai baht continued to fall, so interest rates had to rise further than they would have needed to if the Bank of Thailand had stuck to its guns in the first place. The Thais were not unique in undermining confidence in their own program: Mexico reduced interest rates too quickly in January 1995, President Suharto signalled a lack of determination to pursue agreed reforms in Indonesia and a presidential candidate in South Korea threatened to renegotiate its program after elections there. In contrast Brazil raised interest rates to defend its currency without a Fund program, reducing rates subsequently but only after tightening fiscal policy. Mussa argued that some firming in fiscal policy was called for in all the Asian crisis countries. But he noted that even if the management had not wanted a tightening, the IMF's Executive Board - and especially its creditor country members - would never have approved a program without one.

On monetary policy, Mussa conceded that raising interest rates could worsen the condition of weak financial systems. But he added that interest rates could not be be left alone. He pointed out that the IMF was not dogmatic on this point, and that it had been consistent in urging Japan to run a loose monetary policy. But in Japan's case depreciation would not worsen the balance sheet position of the corporate sector because it was a net creditor. Halting a free fall in the currency is clearly important when banks and corporates in the affected country have large foreign-currency obligations due for repayment within a short period. How much to increase interest rates in crisis countries is clearly a difficult question: given the need to be consistent, there is no point raising them to a level from which the markets know they will soon have to be reduced. Sweden's unsuccessful attempt to use 500% overnight rates to stabilise the kroner during the 1992 ERM crisis stands out as an obvious example.

But Goldstein argued that when investors lose confidence in a currency and attach a high probability to further declines, it is difficult to induce them to hold that currency without higher interest rates. This will depress the economy, but it is unreasonable to expect to overcome a currency and banking crisis without some slowdown: typically in emerging market crises it takes two years for growth to return to pre-crisis levels. Wyplosz argued, however, that as the Asian crisis victims should suffer only a temporary blip in their growth performance it was sensible to smooth consumption through the episode and not to tighten policy unnecessarily. He conceded that this would cause problems for firms with foreign obligations if the exchange rate continued falling, but that this was an argument for a standstill in debt repayments rather than contractionary macroeconomic policies. Goldstein responded in turn that the 'blip' in Latin America's growth performance in the 1980s had lasted a decade and that securing reform was more important than smoothing consumption.

The IMF has also been criticised for demanding the closure of troubled financial institutions, on the grounds that this further undermines confidence in the financial system and impedes recovery. Hale has argued, for example, that the decision to close 16 banks in Indonesia caused such severe liquidity problems in the banking system that it was unrealistic to expect the sort of rise in interest rates that might stabilise the currency.

On this point Mussa draws on the example of the US in 1933, when President Roosevelt called a bank holiday from which 7,000 of the nation's 25,000 banks never returned. He points out that the strongest cyclical recovery in US economic history began a month later. Mussa argued that it was not bank closures per se that damaged confidence, but the fear that more closures would follow in the future. This suggests that the authorities should be decisive in closing insolvent banks and that they could proclaim and guarantee the solvency of those that remain. Goldstein also warns that if insolvent banks are allowed to continue operations, they will be tempted to 'gamble for resurrection' by taking on higher risks that will raise the ultimate resolution cost to the public sector. Bank runs can be desirable if depositors shift funds from weak to strong institutions, as happened in Argentina after the Mexican crisis. But to keep credit contraction under control it is important to ensure that the relatively strong banks have sufficient capital to meet regulatory requirements without a fire-sale of assets.

Miller pointed out that good banks can be encouraged to buy bad ones in lifeboat or convoy operations, but that in a competitive environment they may be reluctant.

Another critique of the IMF's performance in Asia - advanced by Martin Feldstein at Harvard - is that the institution has exceeded its traditional task of helping countries to cope with temporary shortages of foreign exchange and sustained trade deficits, by imposing significant structural and institutional reforms. The reforms imposed on Thailand and Indonesia are more like those the Fund has been imposing in Russia than the largely macroeconomic prescriptions applied in Latin America in the 1980s. 'Although such changes may be desirable in many ways, past experience suggests that they are not needed to maintain a flow of foreign funds', Feldstein argues. 'A nation's desperate need for short-term financial assistance does not give the IMF the moral right to substitute its technical judgements for the outcomes of the nation's political process'.

The World Bank has traditionally been seen as the vehicle for promoting structural reform, but Folkerts-Landau argued that its performance in Asia had been 'wholly ineffective'. He said that it had been very slow in the field, that its activities were not coordinated with those of the Fund and that its performance was almost an embarrassment. The internal restructuring at the Bank did not provide an adequate excuse. Stiglitz argued that it was unrealistic to expect the Bank to move as quickly as the Fund. The sorts of microeconomic reforms that it was involved in required more thought and could not be up and running in a few days. He noted that the Bank's program in South Korea would be substantial, but that the institution was naturally reluctant to come forward with money until it had a clear idea of what it wanted to do in a particular situation. Stiglitz argued that the Bank would have to look closely at the provision of social safety nets, which were important because of the lack of unemployment insurance. The threat of social instability would make the task of economic reform much more difficult.

b). Moral Hazard, Bailouts and Workouts

The critique of the IMF's rescue packages in Asia that is doing most to give policy-makers sleepless nights is the concern over 'moral hazard': the problem that insurance or assistance from official sources encourages risk-taking and results in too many resources flowing into the insured activities in the future. Investors spared pain as a result of multilateral intervention, it is argued, will be encouraged again to disregard the risks of investing in emerging markets, weakening market discipline. Mussa pointed out, however, that some apparent concern about moral hazard appeared to be motivated more by a dislike of paying out money in the present than any concern to discourage imprudent lending in the future.

Research by Ito and Portes questions whether the Mexican rescue was really necessary to avoid systemic risk and that, if there had been no bailout, whether unwise lending would have flowed into Asia to anything like the same degree over the last couple of years. In the wake of the Mexican crisis, the Group of 10 leading industrial countries addressed the moral hazard issue. They issued a report arguing that 'neither debtor countries nor their creditors should expect to be insulated from adverse financial consequences by the provision of large-scale official financing in the event of a crisis'.

In the Asian crisis, however, although domestic borrowers have suffered and foreign equity holders have suffered, it is not clear that foreign lenders to private sector firms or Asian banks have borne a fair share of the impact. Mexico's financial crisis involved a run on government debt, but even though the Asian crisis has primarily involved private sector debt we have still seen official rescue packages worth more than $120bn.

When the foreign exchange crisis hit South Korea, the first priority was to persuade foreign creditors to roll over existing loans as they came due. The ideal solution in this situation, as Miller pointed out, is for the IMF and the national authorities to keep the creditors engaged by guaranteeing that they will be repaid, while promising simultaneously that this will be the last time that such guarantees will be provided. But this solution falls foul of a 'time inconsistency' problem: it is a promise that it is almost impossible to make persuasively. So the response is generally a limited bailout.

To stave off disaster in South Korea without the IMF having to guarantee the repayment of outstanding loans from overseas creditors required the authorities to persuade investors that the country's lack of foreign exchange reserves was only a temporary shortage. Feldstein argues that the IMF's emphasis on the need for substantial structural and institutional reforms achieved the complete opposite. Meanwhile the $57bn rescue package failed to inspire confidence because the IMF had emphasised that it would be disbursed only when the country proved it was conforming to the program. As a result, South Korea's reserves continued to drain away. By late December the IMF and the US agreed to advance $10bn of the agreed finance to forestall default, while the US Federal Reserve and other central banks urged the commercial banks to agree a co-ordinated program of short-term debt rollovers and longer-term rescheduling.

Private sector bankers are generally reluctant to initiate rescheduling themselves because of the fear that offering concessions to one debtor will encourage others to demand similar treatment. When a country has a large number of creditors, there is also a risk that some will act as free riders and exploit sacrifices made by their competitors.

Goldstein presumed that the official reluctance to urge an earlier rescheduling of the short-term debts of Korean banks - and thus to impose a hit on their overseas creditors - reflected a desire not to spread the crisis or to end up with a full-scale debt moratorium. But he argued that this reluctance was also inconsistent with the principles of the G10 report and might have encouraged lenders to channel funds into borrowers deemed 'too large to fail'. Goldstein argued that in future IMF-led rescue packages that involve financial sector restructuring, governments cannot expect earlier announcements of blanket guarantees to be honoured. Instead the treatment of large, uninsured creditors of private firms and banks should be made part of the conditionality attached to IMF programs. Large, uninsured private creditors should stand behind small, insured retail depositors and the insurance fund in the resolution of these institutions' debts.

In the wake of the Mexican crisis, Eichengreen and Portes recommended new institutional arrangements to support a more efficient market-based resolution of sovereign debt crises. By the time the Asian crisis struck, however, nothing had come of these 'orderly workout' initiatives. Even though the Asian crisis has been one of private rather than sovereign debt, Eichengreen and Portes believe that their post-Mexico proposals remain relevant. The reluctance of lenders to roll over loans to the private sector quickly developed into a parallel reluctance to roll over loans to the government on the grounds that the crisis in the private sector might weaken the government's revenue position and, more importantly, that the government might assume responsibility for private sector debts. This threatens a double bailout, in which the IMF bails out domestic governments and foreign lenders, while the domestic government bails out private firms.

Eichengreen and Portes continue to recommend that government bond contracts should include provisions to deal with collective action problems among creditors. Sharing clauses and majority voting clauses would help prevent renegade creditors from hindering rescheduling. The G10 hoped for a 'market-led' movement in this direction, but this has been stymied by the reluctance of industrial country governments to put any provisions in their bond contracts that might hint at the possibility of renegotiation.

Portes and Eichengreen also recommend the creation of standing steering committees for creditors, designed to facilitate better representation and smooth negotiations. But bankers believe that these might be an invitation to rescheduling, making it too easy for borrowers to wriggle out of loan contracts. Their paper also looked at the possibility that Article 8.2(b) of the IMF's Articles of Agreement might be amended to allow the Fund to impose a standstill and shelter countries initiating debt negotiations from legal action. Portes noted that the de facto debt standstill imposed by Indonesia had been greeted surprisingly well by the markets. But Eichengreen argued that this was probably a step too far towards an international bankruptcy procedure, without the ability to impose sanctions on management that existed in the equivalent private sector arrangements. In a related proposal, the G10 said that the IMF should consider lending to countries that had not cleared their arrears, but Miller argued that this threatened legal problems for the Fund which could find itself hauled into court if it helped countries not to pay their debts. Miller argued that the Fund should be authorised to impose a standstill.

3. Prevention

a). Early Warning Indicators

Banking and currency crises are extremely costly for the countries involved. Since the 1980s there have been more than a dozen banking crises in developing countries where the resolution costs have been at least 10% of GDP. Banking crises also deepen recessions, prevent saving from flowing to its most productive uses, constrain monetary policy and increase the likelihood of currency crises. It is hardly surprising, therefore, that policy makers and financial market participants have become increasingly interested in early warning indicators that would identify vulnerability to crises before they strike.

Relying on financial market indicators is not enough. Interest rate spreads gave no indication of the problems looming in Indonesia, Malaysia or the Philippines and provided only intermittent signals for Thailand. Neither were there warnings for Indonesia from the foreign exchange market or the spreads between corporate and government bonds. The sovereign ratings provided by credit rating agencies also tend to be a lagging indicator of problems rather than a leading one. The financial markets and the credit rating agencies may be performing poorly because of a lack of current and comprehensive information on the creditworthiness of a borrower, for example if the true state of a country's foreign exchange reserves is masked by forward commitments.

In his work on early warning indicators with Carmen Reinhart, Goldstein uses macroeconomic indicators to build up a set of signals - the more of which are flashing, the more likely is a crisis. The signal variables were chosen by looking at a sample of 25 emerging market and smaller industrialised countries with a presence in international financial markets. A banking crisis is defined in terms of bank runs, closures, mergers or public sector takeovers of important institutions, while a currency crisis was identified when a weighted average of nominal exchange rate depreciation and loss of reserves moved three or more standard deviations from its mean. On these definitions the sample countries experienced 120 crises between 1970 and 1996, three-quarters of which were currency crises. Defining the period within which a warning can be described as 'early', Goldstein and Reinhart chose 1-24 months in advance for currency crises and 1-12 months before or after for a banking crisis (because banking crises frequently last 4-5 years with the peak often falling several years after it has begun).

Goldstein and Reinhart selected 25 leading indicators, looking for an optimal threshold for each that would maximise the number of accurate crisis signals and minimise the number of false ones. Threshold values differ for each country, so the behaviour of each indicator and the crisis history of each country had to be taken into account. For example, it has taken a larger drop in exports or equity prices to signal that a currency crisis is likely in Mexico than it has in Malaysia or Sweden. To assess when a crisis is likely, you look at the number of indicators that have reached their optimal threshold, weighted by their past forecasting performance. If country A has 20 indicators 'flashing' and country B only 12 indicators flashing, then a crisis is more likely in country A as long as the indicators have been equally reliable in each country.

The better leading indicators predicted between 80-100% of banking and currency crises correctly between 1970 and 1995, sounding on average one false alarm for every two correct ones. The best monthly leading indicators of banking crises were an upward deviation of the real exchange rate from trend, a fall in equity prices, a rise in the money multiplier, a drop in real output, a fall in exports and a rise in the real interest rate. The best monthly indicators of currency crises are real exchange rate appreciation, the presence of a banking crisis, a stock market decline, a fall in exports, an increase in the ratio of M2 to international reserves and a decline in international reserves. The best annual indicators of currency crises were the current account deficit relative to GDP and investment. The best annual indicators of banking crises were the ratio of short-term capital inflows to GDP and the current account deficit relative to investment.

Neither interest rate spreads nor changes in credit ratings perform as well as the best indicators of economic fundamentals, according to Goldstein and Reinhart. Their model showed plenty of red lights flashing for South Korea and Thailand ahead of their recent crises and slightly fewer for Malaysia and the Philippines. The model also predicted last year's Czech crown crisis well, but not the Indonesian crisis. Goldstein and Reinhart would like to add contagion into their model, to incorporate the institutional characteristics of weak banking systems, to investigate the use of composite leading indicators (reflecting the fact, for example, that a rise in interest rates is more problematic for a highly indebted country than a less indebted one) and to update their database to predict which countries are most vulnerable to crises now.

Instead of using a signals approach, Manmohan Kumar and William Perraudin used a multi-variate regression to quantify the probability of a crisis. They focused on currency crises, defining them as episodes in which an unexpected percentage depreciation in a particular currency exceeded a given cut-off point, where the expected depreciation is determined by the differential between domestic and overseas interest rates. In some cases it is difficult to derive a free market interest rate, in which case a crisis is assumed to occur if the depreciation exceeds the given threshold and the rate of decline has accelerated since the previous period. They examined monthly data for 32 emerging market countries since January 1985. Like Goldstein and Reinhart, they found that overvalued exchange rates, falls in exports and recessions were good predictors of currency crises, as they turned out statistically significant in the regressions. Falling commodity prices and declines in portfolio investment were also useful predictors, but they could not generate a statistically significant role for contagion effects.

The estimated probability of a currency crisis in Thailand (defined as an unexpected 5% depreciation over one mnth) rose sharply from around 5% between mid-1995 and mid-1996 to 40% by the spring of 1997. It stood at 45% when the baht was devalued. Falling portfolio investment and weak economic growth were the most important factors leading to a rise in the probability of a crisis through 1997. Their model predicted 80% of crises and gave two or three true signals of a crisis for every false one. Between September 1996 and September 1997, Thailand recorded the biggest rise in the probability of a crisis, followed by the Philippines, Zimbabwe, Korea and Morocco.

Axel Weber noted that different studies had looked at a wide range of potential early warning indicators and that more than 40 of them had turned out to be statistically significant in at least one study. He noted that both the signals and regression approaches were in effect looking for repeating patterns, which was only helpful to the extent that crises were alike rather than idiosyncratic. He noted that the sources of crises appeared to have changed from decade to decade. Eichengreen wondered how useful the Goldstein model would be if one in three of its crisis predictions turned out to be false alarms. Mussa argued that spotting 80% of crises would be a great advance even if one in three signals was false, but Jim Rollo argued that this would not be good enough if the IMF wanted to be confident enough to issue a public warning.

b). Surveillance and the IMF

Mexico's unforeseen financial crisis in 1994-5 prompted a re-evaluation of the IMF's surveillance of national economic policies, which takes place largely through the annual Article Four consultations and in the twice-yearly *World Economic Outlook* exercise. The Fund commissioned a report from Sir Alan Whittome which criticised the surveillance process and resulted in many more resources being devoted to it.

Folkerts-Landau argued that the IMF could not be accused of failing to see the Asian crisis coming. He said that the Fund had warned the national authorities 'forcefully and repeatedly' that policies needed to be changed, but that they were ignored. He noted that when a mission to South Korea was organised for April 1997, the country's representative on the IMF's Executive Board had objected to the presence of a member of the financial sector division on the mission team. The management insisted and South Korea was warned clearly that its financial system was in urgent need of reform.

In recent research, Ito and Portes take a rather less charitable view of the IMF's predictive performance in Asia. They argue that the IMF's Annual Report in December 1996 raised no suspicions and that its 1997 Annual Report found no fault with macroeconomic management in either Thailand or South Korea. The IMF's latest report on International Capital Markets, released in September 1997, devoted only 5 out of 265 pages to the Asian currency crisis and contained no warnings of possible contagion.

There has been a long-running debate within the IMF's management and membership about the relative importance of transparency and confidentiality in surveillance. Advocates of transparency argue that it is only when the Fund is prepared to speak out in public that the more reluctant governments will take its advice seriously. But advocates of confidentiality argue that national authorities will no longer give the IMF useful but sensitive information if they know it is going to be public. There is also the danger that a public warning might precipitate the very crisis it is supposed to prevent.

Folkerts-Landau favoured a more open and confrontational model of surveillance in which the Fund communicates its concerns to the public and the markets quickly. He conceded that this would reduce the amount of information that the national authorities gave the Fund, but argued that this would be a price worth paying. He believes that the extra information that the Fund receives is not very useful and that private sector investors and credit rating agencies get more up-to-date information than does the Fund. Financial market participants also have a better feel for short-term financial flows.

Goldstein argued that the IMF's special data dissemination standards also need beefing up in the wake of the Asian crises. He argued that there ought to be stiffer reporting and public disclosure requirements for the maturity and currency denomination of external debt, for international reserves (net of official commitments in the forward exchange market) and for non-performing loans in the banking system. Better publicly available information on these variables might help to bring corrective market pressure to bear before a crisis has chance to develop. If it was not thought suitable for the special data dissemination standard, the non-performing loan information could be covered in the Basle Committee's 'Core Principles of Effective Banking Supervision'.

In a recent paper, Ito and Portes outline a number of other principles to help borrower countries avoid or minimise crises:

• Do not liberalise capital flows prematurely and indiscriminately, as Korea was encouraged to do on joining the OECD. Be wary of short-term capital inflows, especially foreign currency borrowing by banks and corporates. Consider market-based discouragements or prudential regulations on inflows, such as those used by Chile. Wolf argued that it was difficult to understand why countries with domestic savings ratios as high as Asia's should allow any foreign borrowing, but Eichengreen responded that South Korea had successfully used foreign borrowing to smooth investment and encourage growth for years. It also disciplined domestic borrowers.

- Countries should also accommodate persistent long-run inflows of capital by dismantling restrictions on foreign direct investment.

- If an exchange rate peg is being used to stabilise an economy, think early about how to exit from it. If countries wait until a nominal peg is attacked, it will be too late to avoid a crisis by floating. Countries should move earlier to some sort of managed float, such as a crawling band basket peg.

- Strengthen financial systems, including their regulation and supervision. Beware weak bank balance sheets. To avoid large non-performing loans, use restrictive policies such as a cap on the loan-to-value ratio in the real estate sector.

Summary and Conclusions

Asia's financial crisis has prompted sharp falls in equity prices and exchange rates in the region, the economic implications of which are yet to feed through fully. Thailand, Indonesia and South Korea are facing outright recessions this year, notwithstanding substantial packages of international financial support. In the countries with which they trade, economic growth will slow and current account deficits will widen as the crisis countries export their way to recovery. Resurgent protectionism remains a threat.

The Asian crises are difficult to explain with traditional economic models. Government policies have not been particularly profligate and unemployment has not been high enough to encourage expectations of looser policy in the future. The story is one of unsustainable bubbles in asset prices, fuelled by inflows of private sector capital into economies with weak and poorly regulated financial systems. As in the US Savings and Loans debacle, lenders were encouraged to pump money into financial intermediaries in these countries by implicit guarantees that they would be repaid if things went wrong. This and other features of so-called 'crony capitalism' cannot explain the timing of the crises, but they help to explain both their breadth and severity. The authorities in the crisis countries made matters worse for themselves and the international community, by engaging in last-gasp defences of their fixed exchange rate regimes that increased the eventual cost of resolution when these defences failed. The crisis spread from country to country as the initial problems in Thailand exposed similar weaknesses elsewhere.

As conditions attached to the promises of international financial support, the IMF has imposed its traditional macroeconomic prescriptions - tight monetary policy, fiscal consolidation and the closure of troubled financial institutions. These prescriptions have been controversial. Critics argue that contractionary policies are inappropriate and counterproductive in economies with budget surpluses, low inflation and high savings. Closing banks meanwhile undermines confidence and exacerbates any underlying credit crunch. This, they argue, explains why the announcement of IMF programs failed to restore financial market confidence and shore up the affected countries' exchange rates.

The fiscal policy imposed under the programs may indeed have been unnecessarily tight, but it is not clear that the monetary policy was. More likely confidence was undermined when the authorities backed away from the policy tightening too quickly, which the markets may have taken as a signal that longer term structural reforms were unlikely to be pursued consistently either. In the case of policy towards bank closures, the fault may have been that they were not closed early enough and that not enough was done to re-establish confidence in the solvency of the institutions that remained.

As with the Mexican rescue package before it, the promises of financial assistance in Asia have raised the question of moral hazard. Foreign lenders to Asian corporates and banks have taken much less of a hit than foreign equity holders, which may encourage them to engage in excessive risky lending in the future. The G10 argued after Mexico that 'neither debtor countries nor their creditors should expect to be insulated from adverse financial consequences by the provision of large-scale official financing in the event of a crisis'. More needs to be done to ensure that this is the case.

To avoid moral hazard, IMF programs should make it clear that any blanket guarantees offered to lenders by the affected governments should not be expected to be honoured. But it is unrealistic to expect governments to accept the failure of core institutions. The international community should also be prepared to encourage the private sector to reschedule a country's short-term borrowing earlier than it did in the Asian countries.

Given the way in which private sector debt was in effect taken onto the public sector balance sheet in Asia, there remains a strong argument to push ahead with the 'orderly workout' agenda for sovereign debt that was put forward after Mexico. Industrial country governments should take the lead in agreeing together to insert majority voting and sharing provisions in their bond contracts, so that emerging market countries can be encouraged to do so too. The international community should also re-examine the possibility of allowing the IMF to sanction debt standstills, although this may be seen as too big a step down the road to an international bankruptcy procedure.

Banking and currency crises are costly both for the countries directly affected and also in some cases for the international community, so it is hardly surprising that policy-makers and financial market participants would like to know where they are likely to strike next. A variety of studies have attempted to devise early warning indicators for crises, based on the macroeconomic and other factors which appear to have been associated with crises in the past. The best predictors of crises appear to be real exchange rate overvaluation, falls in exports and recessions, although an enormous range of indicators has been found to be statistically significant in one study or another. These models seem able to predict 80% or more of crises, but with one false alarm for every two or three correct signals. This is an advance on the current state of knowledge, but may not be reliable enough to justify public warnings. Crises all share common features, but each is different in its own way. So any model based on the features of past crises can only be reliable up to a point - crises will always be with us.

The IMF's surveillance of national economic policies was tightened up in the wake of Mexico's financial crisis, which surprised international institutions and financial market participants alike. The IMF did see the Asian crisis coming, especially in Thailand where the denouement began. The authorities were warned to take action in private and in public, although the impact of the public warnings was tempered by the traditional courtesies which the IMF feels it has to adopt when commenting on the policies of its member governments. In future the IMF should perhaps sacrifice some courtesy in favour of greater clarity. This may reduce the amount of sensitive information that national authorities provide the IMF with, but this is probably a price worth paying. In some ways, financial market participants and credit rating agencies have better and more up-to-date information than the Fund. If the national authorities find themselves 'gambling for resurrection', the IMF and the markets alike may be in the dark.

As the lessons of Asia are digested, other emerging market countries will want to know how best they can avoid similar problems. Capital flows can obviously pose problems, but they serve a useful economic purpose and should not be restricted unduly. Having said this, countries should not liberalise capital flows indiscriminately and they should be wary of foreign currency borrowing by their banks and corporates. The costs and benefits of limited capital controls, like those in Chile, deserve closer investigation. Inflows in the form of foreign direct investment should be encouraged. Exchange rate pegs should only be used temporarily to stabilise an economy and countries should endeavour to extricate themselves from them in times of calm before damaging speculation has a chance to build up. Financial systems should also be strengthened so that economies are better able to cope with capital flows and to withstand high interest rates when these are required for the purposes of macroeconomic management.

References

Krugman, P. (1998) 'What Happened to Asia?', html://web.mit.edu/krugman/www/DISINTER.html,   January 1998.

Davies, G. (1998) *Causes, Cures and Consequences of the Asian Economic Crisis*, Goldman Sachs, London, February 1998.

Goldstein, M. 'The Asian Financial Crisis', Institute for International Economics Working Paper, Washington DC (forthcoming).

Eichengreen, B. and Portes, R. (1995) *Crisis? What Crisis? Orderly Workouts for Sovereign Debtors*, Centre for Economic Policy Research, London, 1995.

Goldstein, M. and Reinhart, C. *Forecasting Financial Crises: Early Warning Signals for Emerging Markets*, Institute for International Economics, Washington DC (forthcoming).

Ito, T. and Portes, R. (1998) 'Dealing with the Asian Financial Crises' (forthcoming in *European Economic Perspectives*, Centre for Economic Policy Research, London).

Feldstein, M. (1998) 'Refocusing the IMF', *Foreign Affairs,* April 1998.

Group of 10 (1996) *The Resolution of Sovereign Liquidity Crises, Basle*, May 1996

A New Approach to Managing Financial Crises

Barry Eichengreen & Richard Portes

One predictable consequence of the Asian crisis will be to relaunch the debate about managing these problems. In particular, there will be a clamour for a third alternative to bailouts and inaction. Rescues of the sort mounted on behalf of Thailand, Indonesia, and South Korea have been criticized for aggravating problems of moral hazard. Investors spared a haircut as a result of multilateral intervention, it is said, will be encouraged to again disregard the risks of investing in emerging markets, weakening market discipline. At the same time, the severity of the Asian crisis serves as a powerful reminder that neither can policy-makers simply stand idly by. The notion that markets left to their own devices can sort out the problem is now even less plausible than before. To cite one example, the problems of collective action that arose when banks were asked to roll over their credits to South Korea provides a potent reminder that asymmetric information and the incentive to free ride can be major obstacles to achieving an efficient market solution. The virulence of the contagion reminds us that a country cannot be left to sort out its problems any more than a speeding motorist can be ignored on the grounds that he will suffer the consequences of his own recklessness, for in both cases any misstep can also affect innocent bystanders. However compelling are the critics of the IMF and G-7 when they emphasize the moral-hazard costs of international rescues, their critiques are of little practical value when the only alternative they offer is inaction.

The Asian crisis may have turned the spotlight on these issues, but it is not the first time they have been raised. In the wake of the Mexican crisis, it was agreed that while prevention was the better part of cure, it might not always be possible to prevent financial crises. Even strong warnings by the IMF and others participating in the process of multilateral surveillance, it was agreed, will not always ensure that the markets draw back gradually and that governments smoothly implement the needed policy corrections. Thailand's crisis has now underscored this point. Sometimes a crisis may take even well-informed observers by surprise; for example, few observers, however much they now proclaim the accuracy of their 20-20 hindsight, saw the Korean crisis coming. Certainly more information can only help, but in 1997 the problem was not so much that the markets lacked information as that the unfolding crisis led them to draw rather different inferences from the same information. Crisis avoidance is key, but crises will still occur, notwithstanding policy-makers' best efforts, and there remains the need for better ways of containing them.

Following the Mexican crisis there was widespread recognition that it might not be feasible for the IMF to ride to the rescue of all countries experiencing financial crises. Even financial packages of \$50bn and more might not suffice for countries whose external liabilities are several times greater than this amount. Similarly, there was recognition that, even where this was feasible, preventing all losses on international investment was not desirable, given the moral hazard consequences. At that time two reports (Eichengreen and Portes (1995) and the Group of Ten (1996)) discussed the need to build new institutions to support a more efficient market-based resolution of debt crises and the need for new policy approaches. But when the Asian crisis struck, nothing had yet come of these 'orderly workout' initiatives.

This paper revisits this earlier discussion in light of the Asian crisis. Recent events reinforce previous themes, but they also shed new light on the orderly-workout debate. The Mexican crisis involved a run on the government's bonded debt and prompted proposals for more efficiently restructuring securitized sovereign debt. The Asian crisis, in contrast, involves bank loans, as well as bonds, and private, as well as public, liabilities. This raises the question of whether previous proposals are still pertinent.

We argue that this is indeed the case. While the problem in Asia initially involved the non-sovereign obligations of banks and corporations, it also gave rise to a series of sovereign liquidity crises. The reluctance of lenders to rollover loans to the private sector quickly developed into a parallel reluctance to rollover loans to the government on the grounds that the crisis in the private sector might weaken the government's revenue position and, more importantly, that the government might end up assuming responsibility for many of those same private-sector obligations. There was a perception that the widespread inability of banks and corporates to service their external debts might force a generalized standstill and the imposition of exchange controls, interrupting debt-service payments on sovereign obligations. For all these reasons, the earlier debate around the idea of orderly workouts for sovereign debtors is still relevant.

Although bank loans were significant in Asia, bonds continue to be important as well. The deregulation of securities markets and emergence of a large, liquid secondary market has made bond issuance an attractive vehicle for international lending. The flow of international sovereign bond issues by developing countries (including the transition economies) rose from some $2.5bn a year in the second half of the 1980s to nearly $40bn in 1996, a year when bank loans to sovereigns were no more than $3bn. Perhaps more relevant for this discussion, the *stock* of such bonds reached nearly $250bn at the end of 1996.

We therefore review the case for new provisions in loan contracts (sharing clauses, majority voting clauses) to better deal with collective action problems on the part of creditors; the arguments for and against standing steering committees of creditors designed to facilitate better representation and smooth negotiations; the debate over IMF lending into arrears; and the possibility of amending Article 8.2(b) of the IMF Articles of Agreement to allow the Fund to shelter countries initiating debt negotiations from legal action. We then turn to the case of private sector (bank and corporate) debts, reviewing proposals for more orderly workouts of private debts. On the sovereign debt front, the case for new provisions in loan contracts and standing steering committees of creditors is strongest, but concerted action by national regulators and multilateral institutions would be required to overcome the 'pre-nuptial agreement problem' that prevents any one country from moving first. On the private debt front, most of the necessary steps can be taken at the national level through the adoption of efficient, transparent bankruptcy statutes and the strengthening of independent judiciaries, provided the government does not bail out private sector debtors, but rather leaves them to workouts with their foreign creditors.

References

Eichengreen, B. and Portes, R. (1995) *Crisis, What Crisis? Orderly Workouts for Sovereign Debtors*, Centre for Economic Policy Research, London, 1995.

Group of Ten (1996) *The Resolution of Sovereign Liquidity Crises*, Bank for International Settlements, Basle; and International Monetary Fund, Washington DC.

Currency Crisis Contagion and Containment: A Framework

Charles Wyplosz

The paper asserts that, with the exception of Thailand, the crises of 1997 have been self-fulfilling, i.e. not justified by fundamental imbalances. This diagnostic leads to the prescription of very different policies from those adopted as part of the IMF-led rescue.

After Europe in 1992-3 and Latin America in 1994-5, financial crises have affected Asia in 1997. The view that such crises may be self-fulfilling has initially been greeted with scepticism by both academic economists (see, e.g. Krugman (1997)) and by the IMF (see Capital Markets Report (1993)). The Asian crisis has made new converts to this second generation type of crisis models (Krugman (1998), IMF Capital Market Reports (1997)). It has also added to our understanding of what make self-fulfilling crises possible. It is now clear that self-fulfilling crises cannot just happen anywhere at anytime (Obstfeld (1996)). There must pre-exist a source of weakness. Without any weakness at all, there cannot be any crisis - at least that is what our theories say, and what practical experience suggests as well. The weakness should not be too serious for then it is a clear case of bad fundamentals. Self-fulfilling crises occur when the weakness is sufficiently moderate that a crisis is possible, but not necessary. When the crisis occurs, however, the weakness becomes very serious and justifies ex post the crisis.

From one crisis to another we learn how to extend the list of potential weaknesses. The European crises had shown the role of high unemployment in reducing the ability of authorities to repel speculative attacks. The Mexican crisis has shown the dangers of sovereign borrowing in foreign currency. The Asian crisis now leads us to emphasise financial market imperfections (McKinnon and Pill (1997)).

In view of this growing convergence of views in the diagnostic one could have expected a convergence of opinion regarding the proper policy action. Never has the IMF poured so much money in so little time, and never has it been so harshly criticized by a wide majority of the academic profession. Critics lament an unimaginative application of standard conditionality designed for fundamentals-based crises. In that case, when macroeconomic policies are evidently misguided, the IMF is generally right in suggesting that monetary and fiscal policies be made more prudent, possibly even restrictive. When the crisis is of the self-fulfilling type, the proper policy stance may be different. The IMF response is that its first preoccupation is to prevent further contagion. Containment, it is argued, justifies policies which may not be optimal for a particular country but essential for world financial and economic stability. Not only is such an argument a direct violation of Pareto optimality - which should be strictly applied by an international organisation - but it also rests on a particular view on the phenomenon of contagion.

We still know little on contagion, both in theory and practice. Preliminary work, as in Eichengreen et al. (1996), again emphasizes the need to separate fundamental-based from self-fulfilling features. Contagion may occur because one country's crisis affects the fundamentals of another country. Thus it has been argued by Gerlach and Smets (1995) that one country's devaluation reduces the competitiveness of other countries and creates the need for an exchange rate adjustment elsewhere. Such an interpretation could explain the IMF preoccupation with currency depreciation, but contagion itself may have self-fulfilling features. In that case, containment does not necessarily include preventing a depreciation. Contagion leads to self-fulfilling crises when a crisis in one particular country reveals a new source of weakness. This becomes a signal that makes other countries sharing the same weakness suspicious in the eyes of financial markets. When the baht fell because the current account and budget deficits were unsustainable, it *also* appeared that the Thai financial system was fragile and that Thai firms were indebted in dollars. The markets 'discovered' that this situation can quickly turn into a self-fulfilling crisis: if the currency is devalued, indebted banks and firms become bankrupt, which is the ex post 'proof' that the crisis was justified. But if the crisis had not occurred Korean or Indonesian banks and firms would remain as 'healthy' as their counterparts in tens of countries which have not (yet) been spotted by the markets.

The paper develops a simple framework to explore the policy response to a self-fulfilling crisis. It assumes that households, firms, banks and the authorities never violate their budget constraints. A crisis is, thus, not justified on the grounds that some important segments of the economy are insolvent. When the crisis arbitrarily occurs, the exchange rate depreciates and all the agents react still within their budget constraints. Firms which have borrowed abroad face high debt service costs and seek domestic loans. Commercial banks that also borrowed abroad cut down on their domestic loans. The results is a credit crunch which grips the whole economy.

What is the optimal policy response? This paper assumes that the objective must be, first and foremost, to avoid disruption, that is to keep household consumption as close as possible to the pre-crisis path. The deeper is the depreciation the more spending falls in the face of worsening terms of trade. A tight monetary policy which limits the depreciations, as recommended by the IMF, thus seems to work in the right direction.

This argument fails to take into account the credit crunch previously described. The central bank may alleviate the credit crunch by relaxing its stance. It can even completely shield both banks and consumers from the crisis if it undertakes to borrow abroad. This means that the monetary authorities step in and takes over commercial banks, assuming responsibility for all private deposits and bank loans. Thus for the economy to be entirely protected from the effect of the crisis, the IMF must lend –

potentially very large amounts— to the central bank *and* allow the central bank to expand its credit to the economy. The obvious criticism of this policy is that it creates a serious moral hazard problem. Indeed, if banks are simply taken over there is no reason for exerting prudent behaviour and the central bank may have to step in over and over again.

Instead of borrowing abroad, should the monetary authorities just run down their foreign exchange reserves to make up the loss on private (consumer and bank) borrowing and thus reduce the need for a depreciation? The problem is that such a policy implies quasi-fiscal costs as the central bank has to give up its interest-yielding foreign assets while reducing an equivalent amount of non interest-bearing domestic liabilities, i.e. seigniorage. This strategy is only possible if the government or the IMF picks up the cost, which means borrowing abroad for later repayment.

Finally, what would be the effect of a moratorium on external debts? In this framework, it is clear that if existing debts can be rolled over and if these payments correspond to the amounts that would have been borrowed in the absence of an attack, the economy is entirely protected. If the borrowing would have been higher, there remains a crisis, but a much muted one. If there is any penalty attached to the moratorium, this policy does not suffer from a moral hazard problem to the same extent as the previous solutions.

In conclusion, the moratorium emerges as a promising policy. Coupled with supportive domestic macroeconomic policies, it allows a country hit by a crisis to put its house in order and re-start its economy. Then it can honour its debt, including penalties. One intriguing question is why the IMF does not have a moratorium in its standard tool-kit.

References

Eichengreen, B. and Wyplosz, C. (1993) 'Unstable EMS', *Brookings Papers on Economic Activity* (1), pp. 51-124.

Eichengreen, B., Rose, A. and Wyplosz, C. (1996) 'Contagious Currency Crises' *Scandinavian Economic Review* 98 (4), pp.463-84.

Gerlach, Stefan and Smets (1995).

Krugman, P. (1997) 'Are Currency Crises Self-Fulfilling?', *NEBR Macroeconomic Annual* (1997).

Krugman, P. (1998) 'What Happened to Asia?' MIT (unpublished).

McKinnon, R. and Pill, H. (1997) 'Overborrowing, A Decomposition of Credit and Currency Risks', Stanford University (unpublished).

Obstfeld, M. (1996) 'Models of Currency Crises with Self-Fulfilling Features', *European Economic Review*, April 1996, pp. 1037-47.

Assessing Emerging Market Currency Risk

Manmohan Kumar & William Perraudin

This paper develops a methodology for quantifying currency risk in emerging markets and provides estimates of probabilities of crises for a large sample of countries. The probabilities are computed taking into account a range of country specific economic, financial and political variables as well as global factors. The methodology involves first specifying a variety of econometric models of currency crises. A number of different definitions of crisis are employed. These include devaluations exceeding various thresholds, adjusted for expected devaluation using ratios of domestic and foreign interest rates. Alternative specifications and functional forms are employed, and contagion or 'spillover' effects taken into account. The results of estimation are then used to compute the probabilities of future crises.

Currency crises may reflect the fact that macro fundamentals, financial factors and economic policies are inconsistent with the prevailing exchange rate. Even if this is not the case, expectations of a currency realignment, based for instance on investor beliefs regarding the needs of the real economy, may lead to pressure and crises. The crisis risk framework we develop is consistent with either mechanism. Our specifications are influenced by the growing empirical literature in this area (see references below). We explicitly model the possibility of 'contagion' or spill-over effects from one currency to another. Several channels for spill-overs are taken into account: competitiveness effects, similarity in underlying factors, perceived similarity in economic or financial weaknesses and sentiment driven factors.

The sample consists of 32 emerging market economies from the five regions Asia, Latin America, Eastern Europe and FSU, Middle East and Africa. Over 50 explanatory variables are considered. These variables can be classified into twelve categories, including activity variables; monetary, fiscal and financial factors; current and capital flows and debt variables; terms of trade and reserves; policy environment; global output; liquidity and financial market variables; commodity prices; and contagion effects. The basic approach employs Logit models to estimate a functional relationship between these variables and crises. We combine time-series information (monthly data from January 1985 to July 1997) with cross-sectional data, effectively pooling the experiences of a large number of countries to model the structure of the currency risk.

A variety of models are estimated: a parsimonious model, which uses a small set of ten country specific and three global variables; a second model which uses the main debt and financial sector variables; and a third model which is a comprehensive model which takes into account a large number of variables in the 12 categories noted above. In addition, debt model for Asian and Latin American regions separately.

The estimated coefficients generally have the correct signs, and are statistically significant. The key determinants of crises are shown to be growth, exports, reserves, real effective exchange rate, portfolio and foreign direct investment inflows, international commodity prices and global liquidity. F-tests reveal high statistical significance for the equations as a whole. Both Type I and Type II errors are examined (of these, the first measures whether the model correctly predicts crises if they occur and the second measures the extent to which the model predicts there will not be a crisis when a crisis does not take place). With a probability cut-off of 1% a month, the model predicted 81% of the crises which occurred (Type I error of 19%) and 70% of the non-crises (Type II error of 30%), which is again highly significant. When the probability cut-off is doubled (to 2% per month), the Type I error increases to 29%, but the Type II error falls to 15%.

The parameter results are used to obtain the evolution of probabilities of crises for the sample of countries. For instance, for Thailand the results show how the probability of crisis began to increase significantly from mid-1996 onwards and, just before the onset of the crisis in July 1997, had exceeded 40%. A similar pattern is found for the other Asean countries, and for Korea. In the case of Mexico, the model also shows a perceptible increase in probabilities in the run-up to the crisis in December 1994. These probabilities continue to increase subsequently, highlighting the ensuing depreciations of the peso. Our findings illustrate the importance of changes in crisis probabilities over and above their absolute levels.

A number of trading strategies are evaluated using different models and different data lags. Significant returns could have been obtained by following a simple trading strategy: which consists of shorting currencies if the relevant crisis probabilities exceed a given value. In computing the returns, we take into account the cost of shorting, as well as the actual depreciation when, and if, it happens. Assuming a holding period of just one month, the results suggest that a trading strategy based purely on the model would have yielded very significant returns. This finding suggests our model outperforms simple interest rate differentials as a predictor of crises. The crisis forecasts it generates should therefore be of considerable interest to financial market participants, regulators and economic policy-makers.

References

Eichengreen, B. et al (1996) 'Contagious Currency Crises' CEPR Discussion Paper No. 1453, August 1996.

Frankel, J. and Rose, A. (1996) 'Currency Crashes in Emerging Markets: Empirical Indicators' NBER Paper 5437, January 1996.

Goldstein, M. 'Early Warning Indicators of Financial Instability in Emerging Economies', presented at Symposium on 'Maintaining Financial Stability in a Global Economy'.

Jackson Hole (1997), Wyoming, August 1997.

Kaminsky, G., Lizondo, S. and Reinhart, C. (1997), 'Leading Indicators of Currency Crises', IMF Working Paper WP/97/79, July 1997.

Kumar, M.S. et al (1993) 'An Extended Scenario and Adjustment Model for Developing Countries', IMF WEO Studies, September 1993.

Early Warning Indicators of Currency and Banking Crises in Emerging Economies

Morris Goldstein

Background

There is ample evidence that when banking and currency crises occur, they can be extremely costly for the countries involved. Since 1980, there have been more than a dozen banking crises in developing countries and recent studies put the cumulative total of bail-out costs at roughly $250bn dollars. On top of these enormous fiscal costs, research suggests that banking crises exacerbate recessions; prevent saving from flowing to its most productive use; adversely constrain the conduct of monetary policy; and increase the likelihood of undergoing a currency crisis. In a similar vein, currency crisis can exact a heavy toll. For example, in the immediate aftermath of its peso crisis (in 1995), Mexico experienced a 6% fall in GDP - its worst recession in five years.

While the Asian financial crisis is still underway, there are already clear signs that it too will leave significant costs in its wake - several of the crisis countries are likely to face bills in excess of 10% of GDP to rebuild their banking systems. In addition, the interaction of huge currency and equity market declines, large exposure to short-term and foreign-currency denominated external debt, and induced corporate bankruptcies and bank closures, is sure to depress economic growth over the next few years.

Projected 1998 growth rates in Emerging Asia have been written down sharply over the past three to six months and the most recent consensus forecast now projects negative growth in Thailand, Indonesia, and South Korea (down from the 7-8% consensus prior to the crisis), and only marginally positive growth in Malaysia and the Philippines.

Early Warning Indicators

There has recently been increased interest in identifying early warning indicators that would permit authorities to recognize vulnerability to a crisis beforehand. This in turn increases the chances that corrective policy measures can be taken in time to pre-empt the crisis. The search for reliable early warning indicators has also been motivated by the accumulating evidence that conventional 'market indicators' of default, currency, and banking risks do not seem to provide much advance warning of such crises.

Preliminary work by Goldstein and Reinhart indicates several interesting findings:

- There are recurring patterns of behaviour in the period leading up to the banking and currency crises. The better leading indicators, though very accurate in prediction (anticipating 80-100% of the banking and currency crises that took place in the 1970-95 period), send on the order of one false alarm for every three correct signals, in terms of adjusted noise-to-signal ratios.

- There is wide variation in performance across the leading indicators - with the most accurate at forecasting tending to send the earliest and most persistent signals of banking and currency crises.

- The best high frequency leading indicators of banking crises are an upward deviation of the real exchange rate from trend; a decline in equity prices; a rise in the money multiplier; a decline in real output; a fall in exports; and a rise in the real interest rate. For currency crises, real exchange rate appreciation: the presence of a banking crisis; a stock market decline; a fall in exports; an increase in the ratio of M2 to international reserves; and a decline in international reserves perform the best: a decline in real output just misses the top group.

- Neither interest rate spreads nor changes in credit ratings perform as well in anticipating banking and currency crises as the best of the indicators of economic fundamentals themselves. This may be because these market variables do a better job of anticipating trouble at the level of individual banks, rather than on a system-wide basis.

- In most crises a high proportion of the leading indicators reach their danger thresholds (usually 50-75%). This suggests that when a country is lurching towards a banking or currency crisis many of the wheels come off at once.

- The signals approach seems to have performed relatively well in anticipating the Asian currency crisis, though there is still room for improvement, most obviously by bringing contagion of financial crises across countries into the model.

Policy Lessons

Early warning models of currency and banking crises are merely another tool for illuminating policy choices and for evaluating the sustainability of current economic policies. If one takes a broader perspective on the Asian financial crisis, three important lessons can be learnt.

First, macroeconomic discipline is a necessary but not a sufficient condition for avoiding financial crises. In particular, in a world of high capital mobility and large net private capital inflows to many emerging economies, neglect of financial-sector reform (including an upgrading of banking supervision to international standards) can be the Achilles Heel of rapid economic development.

While the current financial crisis in Asia had multiple origins (see Goldstein (1998B) and Goldstein and Hawkins (1998)), it would not have happened without widespread financial-sector fragility. It is no accident that financial-sector restructuring and reform has been at the heart of the IMF-led official rescue packages for Thailand, Indonesia, and South Korea. But, on the positive side, when the Asian emerging economies do implement serious reform of their financial sectors there is every reason to suspect that they will again be able to register impressive economic performance.

Second, emerging economies need to be very careful about sticking too long with an overvalued fixed exchange rate. The ASEAN 4 currencies generally followed the US dollar down in the first half of the 1990s and then followed it up (against the Japanese yen) during the 1995-7 period. In the process, they experienced some appreciation of their overall trade-weighted real effective exchange rates. Relative to a ten-year average (1987-97), the appreciation was not huge but it did probably cause some apprehension on the part of international investors. This appreciation came in the context of large current-account imbalances (8% of GDP in Thailand in 1996); a sharp export slowdown in 1996; a shift in Japanese foreign direct investment more toward China; an inventory glut in the global electronics market; and growing oversupply in certain important export industries (e.g. autos, semi-conductors, petro-chemicals, steel).

All things considered, moving toward greater flexibility of the exchange rate at an earlier stage (before the overvaluation becomes large) will be the preferred course of action for most emerging economies in most circumstances.

The final lesson to be learnt is that the composition of foreign borrowing matters a good deal for crisis vulnerability. As suggested earlier, while borrowers can reduce the cost of borrowing by assuming rollover and currency risk, there is accumulating evidence that this strategy is penny wise and pound foolish for most emerging economies. Heavy reliance on short-term, foreign-currency denominated borrowing makes it easier to get into a crisis and tougher to get out of one, and when the costs of the financial crisis are included in the overall calculus, the true cost of this borrowing strategy can be expensive indeed. Even though their overall debt burdens were relatively moderate, by international standards, growing liquidity and currency mismatches (especially in Thailand, Indonesia, and South Korea) set the stage for speculative attacks on currencies and helped turn currency crises into debt crises.

Efforts to improve reporting and disclosure on external debt (perhaps as an amendment to the IMF's Special Data Dissemination Standard) will probably be an element of any G-7 Halifax II package to strengthen the international crisis prevention/crisis management architecture. Even in the absence of international initiatives, it would be in the crisis countries' self interest to set up better surveillance over large unhedged foreign currency positions by banks and their customers.

References

Caprio, G. and Klingebiel, D. (1996) 'Bank Insolvencies: Cross-Country Experience' Policy Research Working Paper No. 1620, World Bank, Washington DC, 1996.

Goldstein, M. (1997) 'The Case for an International Banking Standard Policy Analysis' *International Economics* No. 42, Institute for International Economics, Washington DC, April 1997.

Goldstein, M. (1998) 'Comments on Early Warning Indicators of Financial Crises in Emerging Economies' *Maintaining Financial Stability in a Global Economy*, Federal Reserve Bank of Kansas City, (forthcoming).

Goldstein, M. and Hawkins, J. (1998) 'The Origins of the Asian Currency Crisis', Working Paper, Reserve Bank of Australia, Sydney (forthcoming).

Goldstein, M. and Reinhart, C. (1998) 'Forecasting Financial Crises: Early Warning Signals for Emerging Markets', Institute for International Economics, Washington DC (forthcoming).

Honohan, P. (1997) 'Banking System Failures in Developing and Transition Economies: Diagnosis and Prediction', University College, Dublin (unpublished).

Kaminsky, G. and Reinhart, C. (1996) 'The Twin Crises: The Causes of Banking and Balance-of-Payments Problems', Board of Governors of the Federal Reserve System and the International Monetary Fund, Washington DC, September 1996 (unpublished).

Kaminsky, G., Lizondo, S. and Reinhart, C. (1997) 'Leading Indicators of Currency Crises', Board of Governors of the Federal Reserve System, International Monetary Fund, Washington DC, and the University of Maryland at College Park, February 1997 (unpublished).

Macroeconomic Dimensions of the East Asian Crisis

Joseph Stiglitz

The East Asian crisis raises a number of profound issues. It occurred in the fastest growing region in the world – for the last three decades, GDP per capita has consistently grown at 5% or more annually in Indonesia, Korea, Malaysia, and Thailand. The largest international rescue packages in history, totalling more than $100bn, have failed to stem the problem, which continued to deteriorate significantly in the period following the announcement of the packages. In contrast, capital flows and economic performance resumed in most countries within six months of the onset of the Tequila crisis in December 1994.

The crisis raises several important sets of questions about the macroeconomy. First, what was the role of macroeconomic policy and macroeconomic factors in causing the current crisis? Second, why has macroeconomic policy in the last seven months failed to stem the declines in currencies and continued outflows of capital? What are the direct economic effects of the macroeconomic policy response? What are its effects on confidence? Third, what *ought* to be the role of macroeconomic policy in the solution of the crisis?

Perspectives on the Crisis

The lessons we draw from the crisis depend to a large extent on our understanding of the causes of the crisis itself. Most explanations of the crisis begin with a long list of supposed problems of the East Asian countries. This leads many to the *post hoc ergo propter hoc* fallacy of believing that any problem that existed prior to the onset of the crisis is automatically a cause of the crisis. Some of these 'problems' are inconsistent with the data (e.g. in 1996 Thailand's current account deficit was 7.9% of GDP, but Indonesia's was only 3.3% of GDP and Korea's and Malaysia's were falling and reasonably low). Other 'problems' are not necessary for a crisis (e.g. the Scandinavian countries had financial crises despite their highly transparent economies) or sufficient for a crisis (e.g. other countries had weaker financial systems without experiencing a crisis).

Some of the unconvincing explanations derive from 'market myths' akin to the newspaper headlines that proclaim that currencies traded lower on worries about such and such. Economic science, however, is not newspaper journalism. We should not simply report what the market perceives, even if perceptions are important. Many traders are motivated more by trying to guess the perceptions of other traders, not by an understanding of the underlying fundamentals.

Some policy-makers claim that the market expected or demanded a certain response. But who is the market? There are many market players - including outside investors, inside investors, speculators, and others - with systematically different beliefs, information, and circumstance (especially the composition of their portfolios). In many of the East Asian countries, for instance, capital flight by domestic investors occurred before external investors withdrew their money.

Many of these explanations are also inconsistent with a historical perspective, the observation that the East Asian miracle was real. Any explanation of the crisis has to also be consistent with this past success. Simply listing factors, many of which were present long before the crisis emerged, is not a meaningful causal analysis. Instead, the most persuasive explanations for the change we have observed (from rapid growth to crisis) is a change, either in the world or in the policies of the East Asian countries. Both seem to have played a role. The increased integration of global capital markets, with larger flows and possibly greater correlations of movements across markets, clearly places enormous strains on economies. The crisis also seems to be partly the result of rapid financial liberalization without a commensurate strengthening of regulation and supervision.

The Causes of the Vulnerability in East Asia

The crisis in East Asia is very different from crises experienced by many developing countries in the past. The East Asian countries have all run budget surpluses or minimal budget deficits in recent years (in 1997, Thailand's general government surplus amounted to 1.6% of GDP and Indonesia's was 1.4% of GDP). Inflation, another warning sign that countries are trying to push beyond their capacity, was low and drifting still lower in the months before the crisis.

At the same time, the crisis in East Asia has important parallels with previous crises in developed countries – most recently in the Scandinavian countries, but also with the Great Depression. The Scandinavian countries had fixed exchange rates and their crises followed the build-up of bad banking practices in the wake of financial deregulation, that included the replacement of direct restrictions like credit controls with indirect restrictions like reserve requirements. Furthermore, prior to the crisis the Scandinavian countries had eliminated most of the restrictions on international capital flows.

The current account deficit is the main macroeconomic factor that some people have blamed for the crisis. Leaving aside the question of whether this is even consistent with the data for *all* of the countries, we should ask what the government should have done to control the current account deficits. One of the most natural remedies would have been to increase national savings through tighter fiscal policy. But low saving rates in East Asia were hardly the problem.

Many, however, have described the current account deficits as evidence that the economies were 'overheating'. But note, the most important symptom of an overheated economy – rising inflation – was not present. Indeed, Korea's inflation rate had been brought down from 5.5% (still a low number) to 4% over the year preceding the crisis. The term 'overheated' is used precisely because it suggests a mistake in macroeconomic policy. The government should have 'reduced the heat' that is tightened monetary and fiscal policy.

Tighter monetary policy would have done little to address the problems which stemmed not so much from the level of the borrowing, but from the form it took (short term) and what was done with the funds (speculative and misguided investment). As it was, the *incentives* created by macroeconomic policy were much more important than the *stance* of macroeconomic policy. Government exchange rate policies, either pegging to the dollar or managing the float, encouraged investors to build up unhedged debt. At the same time, the sterilization of capital inflows raised domestic interest rates, encouraging people to borrow from abroad, and possibly causing adverse selection effects that led to more risky investments.

Even with a well functioning financial system, it is likely that these incentives would have led to an aggregate exposure of short-term, foreign-denominated debt. Instead of banks, corporations or non-bank financial institutions would have accessed international markets directly. This is, of course, what happened in Indonesia, where two-thirds of the external bank lending was to the non-bank private sector, among the highest fraction of any country in the world.

The Depth and Duration of the Crisis

Why has the crisis been so much deeper and longer than we expected, at least initially? Part of the answer to this question lies in the initial conditions, the vulnerability of the East Asian economies to a shift in beliefs. These include the high debt-equity ratios of firms, the low capitalization ratios of banks, the high foreign exchange exposure, and the short maturity structure of external debt. Although none of these probably made the crisis inevitable (the overall level of debt, for instance, was sustainable), they did open up the possibility that a shift in beliefs would be self fulfilling.

These, however, are only the initial conditions. We also need to ask about the role of that other changes, especially the macroeconomic policy response, have played in the evolution of the crisis. There is much that we know about this issue but, unfortunately, several crucial issues are still unresolved.

The Policy Response: What We Know

Prior to the outbreak of the crisis, aggregate demand and aggregate supply were roughly in balance. Since the crisis we have seen a major contraction in aggregate demand – a leftward shift of the aggregate demand curve – as consumption and investment have fallen sharply. At the same time, these effects are partly offset by the trade balance. We have seen imports fall sharply from the combined effect of the depreciation and economic downturn, while exports have picked up in some countries – but have still been weaker than many had hoped because of the weaknesses of their trading partners and the lack of credit availability. Overall, however, the direct effect on the macroeconomy of an increase in interest rates or the fiscal surplus would be to further contribute to the weakening of the economy.

At the same time, higher interest rates have important effects at the *microeconomic* level that could constrict aggregate supply at the same time that they reduce the level of aggregate demand. Higher interest rates – higher than had been anticipated when debt was contracted for and when business plans were made – can have significant adverse effects on the economy for several reasons:

- They lower the *net worth* of debtors, probably contracting the economy by more than the expansion in the net worth of creditors. This is especially true when the creditors are external.

- They lead to more *bankruptcies*, which can have a significant adverse effect, especially given the underdeveloped state of bankruptcy laws in East Asia.

- The decrease in net worth may increase *moral hazard*, encouraging firms to engage in gambling or looting behaviour.

- As financial institutions go bankrupt and banks cut back on their lending, credit may become highly constrained. A *credit crunch* may set in, exacerbating the economic downturn.

- Large changes in interest rates increase *uncertainty* about a firm's net worth and other financial characteristics because of the inevitable imperfect information about its asset structure, which interacts with the interest rate to determine the value of the firm. These adverse information effects exacerbate the always present problems of making good resource allocation (lending) decisions, increase risk premia, and thereby contribute further to the contraction of the economy.

These considerations have an important effect on our evaluation of the likely effects of higher interest on capital flows and the exchange rate. The goal of higher interest rates is to increase the rate of return, persuading people to keep their capital in the country. But in a crisis situation we need to ask the deeper question, why are people pulling their money out of the economy in the first place? Often it is because they do not believe that they will receive the promised rate of return, that is, they are worried about the possibility of default.

Higher interest rates increase the *promised* return, but in many circumstances they will also create financial strains, leading to bankruptcies and thus increasing the expectations of default. As a result, the *expected* return to lending to the country may actually fall with rising interest rates, making it less attractive to put money into the economy.

Moreover, even this expected return needs to be adjusted for risk. Policies that increase the likelihood of a major economic downturn inevitably increase the risk premium. Furthermore, while economists rightly focus on the economic consequences of their policies, they cannot ignore the political consequences. We know that there are systematic relationships between economic downturns and political disturbances; and we know that an enhanced likelihood of political disturbances will weaken confidence in the economy.

What We Do Not Know: How to Restore Confidence

Most of our theories and experience with the direct economic effects suggest that higher interest rates and tighter fiscal policy would probably not play a constructive role in responding to the crisis in East Asia. The justification for temporarily tighter monetary policy and contractionary fiscal policy, however, has not rested as much on these direct economic effects as it has on the restoration of confidence. Although restoring confidence is critical, we have little theory and perhaps even less evidence about what will restore confidence.

Addressing this issue systematically requires us to ask what determines individuals beliefs, and how to revise these beliefs. Some economists prefer to answer this in a purely rational framework. Others, like John Maynard Keynes, use terms like 'animal spirits' as a label for the unexplainable component of beliefs.

Higher interest rates could, for instance, be a signal that the government is seriously committed to reform. This seems to have been the case in Latin America. But the origins of the crisis in East Asia were different. Does the market still expect the same remedy? What if its beliefs are wrong? What are the higher interest rates signalling, especially where the commitment of monetary authorities to low and stable inflation was never in doubt?

The signalling effect of higher interest rates can also go the wrong way. Investors believe that a high level of interest rates today will lead to less investment, lower productivity growth, and, consequently, a lower exchange rate in the future; therefore, *at current exchange rates* a larger depreciation. This is particularly true if there are multiple equilibria, and the high interest rates serve to coordinate the market on the weak economy/low exchange rate equilibria.

All of these models are complicated by differences in beliefs. Foreign investors, domestic investors, and speculators may all respond to different policies in different ways. It is possible, for instance, that high interest rates might attract foreign capital, while leading domestic investors to move their money out of the economy in order to diversify against the greater likelihood of a domestic downturn. The overall effect of the policy on the exchange rate and capital flows would then depend on the magnitude of the reactions by these two groups.

The Evidence on the Policy Response

These questions about the direct economic effects and confidence can only be resolved by systematic empirical work. One important preliminary observation is that between 1 July 1997 and 30 January 1998, we have seen exchange rates fall by roughly 40% in Korea, Malaysia and the Philippines; more than 50% in Thailand; and 80% in Indonesia. At the same time, money market interest rates have increased by 10 or more percentage points in all of the countries except Malaysia. By itself, this provides tentative support for the claim that the predominant effect of interest rate increases has been to weaken the economies and thus the currencies, rather than to strengthen the demand for local currency. The natural counter argument, however, is that without the higher interest rates, the depreciations would have been larger.

A more sophisticated version of this same observation is provided by rolling correlations between interest rates and exchange rates. In the initial phase of the crisis, interest rates and exchange rates (defined as dollars per local currency, so that an increase represents an appreciation of the local currency) were negatively correlated, suggesting that the economic effects outweighed the confidence effects. By September 1997, however, the relationship reversed and we began to see higher interest rates being associated with a stronger currency. This relationship did not last very long and by late October the correlations had turned negative again in most of the affected countries. The behaviour of these correlations is somewhat different from Mexico in 1994-5 which was generally characterized by a positive relationship between interest rates and exchange rates.

Conclusion

In the last 15 years there has been a reconstruction of macroeconomic theory, on the basis of sound microeconomic underpinnings, to give an increasing role to the importance of the financial system and its linkages to the rest of the economy. These models have been used to provide insights into events from the Great Depression to the 1990-1 recession in the US. This paper is an attempt to use these ideas to understand the current Asian crisis. The main finding of the paper is that this crisis is very different from many previous, more macroeconomic crises, and that many of the lessons drawn from the experience in those countries are inapplicable to East Asia today.